Practical
Pre-School

Planning for Learning through The Senses

by Judith Harries Illustrated by Cathy Hughes

Contents

Published by Step Forward Publishing Limited

25 Cross Street, Leamington Spa CV32 4PX Tel: 01926 420046
www.practicalpreschool.com
© Step Forward Publishing Limited 2005

Planning for Learning through The Senses ISBN: 1 902438-98-1

Making plans

Why plan?

The purpose of planning is to make sure that all children enjoy a broad and balanced curriculum. All planning should be useful. Plans are working documents that you spend time preparing, but which should later repay your efforts. Try to be concise. This will help you in finding information quickly when you need it.

Long-term plans

Preparing a long-term plan, which maps out the curriculum during a year or even two, will help you to ensure that you are providing a variety of activities and are meeting the statutory requirements of the *Curriculum Guidance for the Foundation Stage* (QCA, 2000).

Your long-term plan need not be detailed. Divide the time period over which you are planning into fairly equal sections, such as half terms. Choose a topic for each section. Young children benefit from making links between the new ideas they encounter so as you select each topic, think about the time of year in which you plan to do it. A topic about minibeasts will not be very successful in November!

Although each topic will address all the learning areas, some could focus on a specific area. For example, a topic on 'The senses' would lend itself well to activities relating to Personal, Social and Emotional Development and Knowledge and Understanding of the World. Another topic might particularly encourage the appreciation of stories. Try to make sure that you provide a variety of topics in your long-term plans.

Autumn 1	Nursery rhymes
Autumn 2	Food/Christmas
Spring 1	Animals
Spring 2	The senses
Summer 1	Sounds
Summer 2	Journeys

Medium-term plans

Medium-term plans will outline the contents of a topic in a little more detail. One way to start this process is by brainstorming on a large piece of paper. Work with your team writing down all the activities you can think of which are relevant to the topic. As you do this it may become clear that some activities go well together. Think about dividing them into themes. The topic of 'The senses', for example, has weekly themes such as 'Seeing eyes', 'Hearing ears', 'Touching hands', 'Smelling noses', 'Tasting tongues' and 'Working together'. At this stage it is helpful to make a chart. Write the theme ideas down the side of the chart and put a different area of learning at the top of each column. Now you can insert your brainstormed ideas and quickly see where there are gaps. As you complete the chart take account of children's earlier experiences and provide opportunities for them to progress.

Refer back to the *Curriculum Guidance for the Foundation Stage* and check that you have addressed as many different aspects of it as you can. Once all your medium-term plans are complete make sure that there are no neglected areas.

Planning for Learning through The Senses   **Practical Pre-School**

Making plans

Day-to-day plans

The plans you make for each day will outline aspects such as:

- resources needed;

- the way in which you might introduce activities;

- the organisation of adult help;

- size of the group;

- timing;

- key vocabulary.

Identify the learning that each activity is intended to promote. Make a note of any assessments or observations that you are likely to carry out. On your plans make notes of activities that were particularly successful, or any changes you would make another time.

A final note

Planning should be seen as flexible. Not all groups meet every day, and not all children attend every day. Any part of the plan can be used independently, stretched over a longer period or condensed to meet the needs of any group. You will almost certainly adapt the activities as children respond to them in different ways and bring their own ideas, interests and enthusiasms. The important thing is to ensure that the children are provided with a varied and enjoyable curriculum that meets their individual developing needs.

Using the book

- Collect or prepare suggested resources as listed on page 21.

- Read the section which outlines links to the Early Learning Goals (pages 4-7) and explains the rationale for the topic of 'The senses'.

- For each weekly theme two activities are described in detail as an example to help you in your planning and preparation. Key vocabulary, questions and learning opportunities are identified.

- The skills chart on page 23 will help you to see at a glance which aspects of children's development are being addressed as a focus each week.

- As children take part in the suggested activities, their learning will progress. 'Collecting evidence' on page 22 explains how you might monitor children's achievements.

- Find out on page 20 how the topic can be brought together in a grand finale involving parents, children and friends.

- There is additional material to support the working partnership of families and children in the form of a 'Home links' page, and a photocopiable parent's page at the back of the book.

It is important to appreciate that the ideas presented in this book will only be a part of your planning. Many activities that will be taking place as routine in your group may not be mentioned. For example, it is assumed that sand, dough, water, puzzles, floor toys and large scale apparatus are part of the ongoing pre-school experience, as are the opportunities which increasing numbers of groups are able to offer for children to develop ICT skills. Role-play areas, stories, rhymes and singing, and group discussion times are similarly assumed to be happening each week although they may not be a focus for described activities.

Using the Early Learning Goals

Having chosen your topic and made your medium-term plans you can use the *Curriculum Guidance for the Foundation Stage* (QCA, 2000) to highlight the key learning opportunities your activities will address. The Early Learning Goals are split into six areas: Personal, Social and Emotional Development; Communication, Language and Literacy; Mathematical Development; Knowledge and Understanding of the World; Physical Development and Creative Development. Do not expect each of your topics to cover every goal but your long-term plans should allow for all of them to be addressed by the time a child enters Year 1.

The following section highlights parts of the *Curriculum Guidance for the Foundation Stage* in point form to show what children are expected to be able to do in each area of learning by the time they enter Year 1. These points will be used throughout this book to show how activities for a topic on 'The senses' link to these expectations. For example, Personal, Social and Emotional Development point 7 is 'form good relationships with adults and peers'. Activities suggested which provide the opportunity for children to do this will have the reference PS7. This will enable you to see which Early Learning Goals are covered in a given week and plan for areas to be revisited and developed.

In addition, you can make sure that activities offer variety in the goals to be encountered. Often a similar activity may be carried out to achieve different learning objectives. For example, during this topic the children will make gingerbread men biscuits. They will be developing Communication, Language and Literacy skills as they respond to the traditional story and act it out using their biscuits. They will also be using Knowledge and Understanding of the World as they observe changes to the ingredients and Personal, Social and Emotional Development as they take turns and make decisions about favourite flavours. It is important, therefore, that activities have clearly defined goals so that these may be emphasised during the activity and for recording purposes.

Personal, Social and Emotional Development (PS)

This area of learning covers important aspects of development that affect the way children learn, behave and relate to others.

By the end of the Foundation Stage, most children will:

PS1   continue to be interested, excited and motivated to learn

PS2   be confident to try activities, initiate ideas and speak in a familiar group

PS3   maintain attention, concentrate and sit quietly when appropriate

PS4   have a developing awareness of their own needs, views and feelings and be sensitive to the needs, views and feelings of others

PS5   have a developing respect for their own cultures and beliefs and those of other people

PS6   respond to significant experiences, showing a range of feelings when appropriate

PS7   form good relationships with adults and peers

PS8   work as part of a group or class, taking turns and sharing fairly, understanding that there needs to be agreed values and codes of behaviour for groups of people, including adults and children, to work together harmoniously

PS9   understand what is right, what is wrong, and why

PS10   dress and undress independently and manage their own personal hygiene

PS11   select and use activities and resources independently

PS12   consider the consequences of their words and actions for themselves and others

PS13 understand that people have different needs, views, cultures and beliefs, that need to be treated with respect

PS14 understand that they can expect others to treat their needs, views, cultures and beliefs with respect

The topic of 'The senses' provides valuable opportunities for children to develop awareness of their own needs and feelings. In particular, time spent meeting people with visual or hearing impairments will encourage children to think about the needs and feelings of others. Opportunities to discuss their senses, share the smelly socks day and go on various walks will encourage children to speak in a group, to share their feelings and to consider consequences. By playing circle games and singing the cuckoo song, children will learn to take turns and to listen to each other. Many of the areas outlined above will also be covered as children carry out activities in other key areas of learning. For example, during undirected free choice times they will be developing PS11 while any small group activity that involves working with an adult will help children to work towards PS7.

Communication, Language and Literacy (L)

The objectives set out in the *National Literacy Strategy: Framework for Teaching* for the Reception year are in line with these goals. By the end of the Foundation Stage, most children will be able to:

L1 enjoy listening to and using spoken and written language, and readily turn to it in their play and learning

L2 explore and experiment with sounds, words and texts

L3 listen with enjoyment and respond to stories, songs and other music, rhymes and poems and make up their own stories, songs, rhymes and poems

L4 use language to imagine and recreate roles and experiences

L5 use talk to organise, sequence and clarify thinking, ideas, feelings and events

L6 sustain attentive listening, responding to what they have heard by relevant comments, questions or actions

L7 interact with others, negotiating plans and activities and taking turns in conversation

L8 extend their vocabulary, exploring the meaning and sounds of new words

L9 retell narratives in the correct sequence, drawing on language patterns of stories

L10 speak clearly and audibly with confidence and control and show awareness of the listener, for example by their use of conventions such as greetings, 'please' and 'thank-you'

L11 hear and say initial and final sounds in words and short vowel sounds within words

L12 link sounds to letters, naming and sounding letters of the alphabet

L13 read a range of familiar and common words and simple sentences independently

L14 show an understanding of the elements of stories such as main character, sequence of events, and openings, and how information can be found in non-fiction texts to answer questions about where, who, why and how

L15 know that print carries meaning, and in English, is read from left to right and top to bottom

L16 attempt writing for different purposes, using features of different forms such as lists, stories and instructions

L17 write their own names and other things such as labels and captions and begin to form sentences, sometimes using punctuation

L18 use their phonic knowledge to write simple regular words and make phonetically plausible attempts at more complex words

L19 use a pencil and hold it effectively to form recognisable letters, most of which are correctly formed

The 'Senses' topic offers various opportunities for children to respond to well-known picture books and stories. By retelling stories, writing poems and making books, children reinforce and extend their vocabulary. Forming letters in trays of different materials, making recipes and menus for the café, and writing invitations will help children to develop their early writing skills. Throughout the topic, children are encouraged to explore the sounds of words and rhymes, to use descriptive vocabulary and to see some

of their ideas recorded in poems, pictures, words and on tape. Role-play areas are described that will allow children to use their imagination as they visit the optician's and buy and sell food at the Tasty Café.

Mathematical Development (M)

The key objectives in the *National Numeracy Strategy: Framework for Teaching* for the Reception year are in line with these goals. By the end of the Foundation Stage, most children should be able to:

M1   say and use number names in order in familiar contexts

M2   count reliably up to ten everyday objects

M3   recognise numerals one to nine

M4   use language such as 'more' or 'less' to compare two numbers

M5   in practical activities and discussion begin to use the vocabulary involved in adding and subtracting

M6   find one more or one less than a number from one to ten

M7   begin to relate addition to combining two groups of objects and subtraction to 'taking away'

M8   talk about, recognise and recreate simple patterns

M9   use language such as 'circle' or 'bigger' to describe the shape and size of solids and flat shapes

M10   use everyday words to describe position

M11   use developing mathematical ideas and methods to solve practical problems

M12   use language such as 'greater', 'smaller', 'heavier' or 'lighter' to compare quantities

As children enjoy the activities in this topic, they will develop mathematical skills in a meaningful context. Estimating, matching, sorting and counting skills are used to play number games with sounds, sweets, bricks and a variety of small objects. A treasure hunt and the game 'Eat the pie' will help children to count and recognise numbers. Following recipes for smelly playdough will help children to use numbers in a practical activity. Simple money skills are introduced in the Tasty Café. Children use mathematical skills to create bar charts showing eye colours and favourite smells. There are many opportunities during water and sand play, especially when making smelly potions, for children to use mathematical language related to measurement and volume.

Knowledge and Understanding of the World (K)

By the end of the Foundation Stage, most children will be able to:

K1   investigate objects and materials by using all of their senses as appropriate

K2   find out about, and identify, some features of living things, objects and events they observe

K3   look closely at similarities, differences, patterns and change

K4   ask questions about why things happen and how things work

K5   build and construct with a wide range of objects, selecting appropriate resources and adapting their work where necessary

K6   select the tools and techniques they need to shape, assemble and join materials they are using

K7   find out about and identify the uses of everyday technology and use information and communication technology and programmable toys to support their learning

K8   find out about past and present events in their own lives, and those of their families and other people they know

K9   observe, find out about and identify features in the place they live and the natural world

K10   begin to know about their own cultures and beliefs and those of other people

K11   find out about their environment, and talk about those features they like and dislike

The 'Senses' theme clearly offers many opportunities for children to investigate objects and materials using all their senses! They can find out about how their senses work, look at their eyes and ears and use their noses to play 'Smelly matching pairs'. They can investigate which part of their body is most sensitive to touch and look closely at their fingerprints. There are opportunities to use tools as they use magnifying glasses and microscopes. Several activities focus on constructing models, including binoculars and feely boxes. They can observe differences and change as they make fizzy sherbet and food for the Tasty Café. Throughout all the activities children should be given the chance to talk about their experiences and ask questions.

Physical Development (PD)

By the end of the Foundation Stage, most children will be able to:

PD1   move with confidence, imagination and in safety

PD2   move with control and coordination

PD3   show awareness of space, of themselves and of others

PD4   recognise the importance of keeping healthy and those things which contribute to this

PD5   recognise the changes that happen to their bodies when they are active

PD6   use a range of small and large equipment

PD7   travel around, under, over and through balancing and climbing equipment

PD8   handle tools, objects, construction and malleable materials safely and with increasing control

Children need to understand and value physical skills and the importance of healthy exercise. A whole range of activities are described to enable children to develop skills and confidence in a fun and exciting way. Several collaborative games, such as 'Blindfold pairs' and 'Follow my leader', offer opportunities to move safely with control and coordination. 'Musical moves' and 'Moving like elephants' give children the challenge to move with imagination. As children join in the breathing exercises they will become aware of how their bodies change when they are active. Children will use a range of equiment such as bean bags, balls, skittles and climbing apparatus. Activities such as using textured playdough and building with large boxes will offer experience of PD8.

Creative Development (C)

By the end of the Foundation Stage, most children will be able to:

C1   explore colour, texture, shape, form and space in two or three dimensions

C2   recognise and explore how sounds can be changed, sing simple songs from memory, recognise repeated sounds and sound patterns and match movements to music

C3   respond in a variety of ways to what they see, hear, smell, touch and feel

C4   use their imagination in art and design, music, dance, imaginative and role play and stories

C5   express and communicate their ideas, thoughts and feelings by using a widening range of materials, suitable tools, imaginative and role play, movement, designing and making, and a variety of songs and musical instruments

During this topic, children will experience working with a wide variety of materials as they design and make fancy spectacles, touch squares, pot-pourri, scratch and sniff cards and musical instruments. They will be able to develop painting skills as they make ink-blot paintings, finger paintings and do press printing with natural and made materials, including fruit and vegetables. They can use perfumed paint, paint self-portraits and even try painting wearing a blindfold! C2 and C5 are explored as the children sing songs and invent sound effects. They can use their imagination in drama activities as they act out the story of 'Little Red Riding Hood'. Throughout all the activities children are encouraged to talk about what they see and feel as they communicate their ideas in painting, collage, music, mime and drama.

Week 1
Seeing eyes

Personal, Social and Emotional Development

- Introduce the theme with a large picture of a child and discuss and label different body parts in relation to the senses. (PS1, 3, 4)

- Play a circle game of 'I spy'. Use colours, shapes, sizes and initial letters. (PS1, 2, 8)

- Invite a partially sighted or blind person to visit with their guide dog and talk to children. Talk about what it might feel like to not be able to see. Which activities would it be difficult to do? If possible, look at some Braille books. Use embossed stamps and coins to make raised patterns. (PS3, 4, 6, 7, 11)

- Read *Lucy's Picture* by Nicola Moon. How did Lucy help her blind Grandpa to see her picture? Make textured pictures to say thank you to your blind visitor. (PS3, 6, 7, 11, 13)

Communication, Language and Literacy

- Set up an optician's in the role-play area (see activity opposite). (L1, 4, 5, 12, 17)

- Read *Duck's Key, Where can it be?* by Jez Alborough. Make up stories about losing something important and having to look everywhere to find it. (L3, 4, 9)

- Make a class book of 'My senses', beginning this week with sight, and add to it throughout the topic. Ask children to draw or cut out pictures of eyes and write or scribe their favourite sights. (L14, 15, 16, 19)

Mathematical Development

- Go on a treasure hunt outside. Give children a list of things to find or spot such as:

3 stones	2 birds
1 feather	4 windows
5 leaves	1 flower

Can they find one more stone? How many have they got altogether? (M2, 3, 6)

- Try some estimating activities (see activity opposite). (M2, 4, 11, 12)

- Play a game with a hand puppet and a set of coloured cards. Use three pairs of red, yellow and blue cards. If the puppet holds up one colour, ask the children to find the matching pair and shout 'snap'. Try the game with matching shape and number cards one to ten. Hide one card. Can the children tell which number or shape is missing? (M1, 2, 3, 9)

Knowledge and Understanding of the World

- Ask children to look carefully at their eyes in hand mirrors. Show them a diagram of the eye and talk about how it works. What do eyelashes do? Why do some people need to wear glasses or contact lenses? (K1, 2, 4)

- Make a collection of tools used for looking at things, such as mirrors, magnifying glasses, a microscope, binoculars, telescope. Help children use them to see how they work. (K1, 2, 3, 4)

- Make binoculars out of cardboard tubes. (K5, 6)

Physical Development

- Play 'Blindfold pairs'. Ask children to work with a partner. Blindfold one of the pair and ask the sighted partner to guide their friend around the equipment. (PD1, 2, 3, 7)

- Practise throwing and catching with different sized balls, skittles and bean bags. Remind children to keep their eye on the ball! (PD2, 6)

Creative Development

- Sing verse one of 'The senses song' to the tune of 'In and out the dusty bluebells'.

  With my two eyes, I can see   x 3

  Using all my senses.

  Add new verses each week, for example: 'With my two ears, I can hear' and so on. (C2)

- Make ink-blot paintings. Drop a pool of very runny paint onto paper and blow with straws to create new shapes. What can children see? Can they turn it into something new? (C1, 3, 4)

- Make fancy spectacles. Cut templates for children to decorate with paint, sequins, beads, feathers, lace, ribbon, fabric, and shiny paper. Display them at the optician's. (C5)

Activity: The optician's

Learning opportunity: Using the role-play corner to share and explore experiences. Writing letters, shapes, colours and numbers and using ICT to make eye charts.

Early Learning Goal: Communication, Language and Literacy. Children will be able to use language to imagine and recreate roles and experiences. They will link sounds to letters, naming and sounding the letters of the alphabet.

Resources: A role-play area set out as an optician's (with a chair, lots of glasses frames, mirrors, torch, computer, telephone, eye charts, posters and brochures about glasses and contact lenses); card; pens; pencils; children's name cards.

Organisation: Whole group introduction with small group using the area.

Key vocabulary: Optician's, eyes, sight, see, letters, numbers, shapes, colours.

What to do:

Talk about going to the optician's for an eye test. Invite any children who have visited the optician's to share their experiences. Involve children in setting up the area. Ask them to make eye charts using lower case and capital letters, simple outline shapes, blocks of colour or numbers. Can they make the rows of letters or shapes start big and get smaller as they move down the page? Encourage children to use a computer to change the style and size of fonts.

Talk about how to use the area. Show children how to try on glasses and read the charts. Warn them not to shine lights or put anything in their eyes, just pretend! Encourage them to take turns at different roles: optician, patient, friend, receptionist.

Activity: How many?

Learning opportunity: Developing, estimating and counting skills.

Early Learning Goal: Mathematical Development. Children will count up to ten everyday objects.

Resources: Cubes; sweets; raisins; clear plastic jar; glass pebbles; different-sized boxes; weights; weighing scales.

Organisation: Small group.

Key vocabulary: Estimate, guess, count, more, less, heaviest, lightest, same, tallest, measure.

What to do:

Show children some cubes (start with under ten) and let them hold them in their hands. Can they guess how many there are? Count the cubes to find out if they are right. Try again with more cubes. Put some glass pebbles on a plate or sweets or raisins in a jar and ask children to estimate how many there are. Do they think there are more or less than ten? Help them to count and check.

Fill a set of different-sized boxes with a variety of weights. Can they tell which is the heaviest just by looking? Let them pick up the boxes and estimate again. Weigh boxes to establish their weights. Begin by making the biggest box heaviest, and the smallest the lightest. Then mix up the contents and try again. The children will find out that they cannot rely on just sight.

Display

On a display table, make a collection of fiction and non-fiction books about senses. Add posters, puzzles and games. This week include lift-the-flap books and those with things to spot! Compile a list of useful words about the senses and display them around the room.

Make a bar chart of eye colours in the group. Help children to cut out pictures of eyes from magazines to stick on the chart. Which is the most common colour?

Under a heading 'What can you see?' leave out the microscope and magnifying glasses for children to use.

Week 2

Hearing ears

Personal, Social and Emotional Development

- Go on a listening walk inside and outside. Can children identify all the sounds? Were there any unexpected sounds? (PS1, 3, 6, 7)

- Record children talking and singing. Can they recognise themselves or identify each other? Play 'The cuckoo song'. Form a circle and ask for a volunteer to sit in the middle wearing a blindfold. Hide a small soft toy bird behind another child's back. All sing 'Cuckoo, where are you?'. The child with the toy replies 'cuckoo'. Can the blindfolded child recognise who sang? (PS2, 3, 8)

- Pass a sound around the circle. Take it in turns to make a sound using voice, body percussion or instruments. (PS3, 8)

- How easy is it to create silence? Imagine what it would be like to not be able to hear any sounds. Teach some simple sign language. (PS3, 4)

Communication, Language and Literacy

- Play a circle game 'I hear with my little ear, something that rhymes with...'. Make a collection of words that rhyme with 'hear'. Make rhyming word chains for other senses words and hang them up on the wall. (L1, 2, 3, 7, 8, 11)

- Make a cosy listening area with comfortable chairs and cushions. Encourage children to listen to story tapes and music. Invite them to talk to the group about what they heard. (L1, 3, 6)

- Hold a large shell up to children's ears and invite them to listen carefully. What can they hear? Help them to write imaginative poems called 'Inside the shell'. (L3, 4, 6, 7, 8)

Mathematical Development

- Play 'Number soundtracks'. Record a series of number puzzles on a tape for children to explore, such as 'Which number comes after four?', 'Point at number seven' and 'Which number is one smaller then three?'. (M2, 3, 4, 5, 6)

- Make a set of matching sound pots. You will need five pairs of black and white film canisters. Fill with coins, rice, beans, sand and lentils. Can children find the matching pairs? (M1, 10, 11)

- Play 'Can you remember?'. Sit in a circle with a group of musical instruments in the middle. Invite a child to choose an instrument to play. Ask them to make a sound on the instrument and then get the next child to repeat it and add one of their own. How many sounds can they remember? (M1, 2, 4, 6)

Knowledge and Understanding of the World

- Investigate how our ears work (see activity opposite). (K1, 2, 3, 4)

- Make a telephone using two plastic cups and a length of string pulled taut. Give children messages to send to each other. What happens if the string is not stretched? Press a plastic funnel into the end of a length of plastic tubing or hosepipe and make a listening tube. Which works best? (K1, 2, 4, 5)

Physical Development

- Play 'Musical moves' (see activity opposite). (PD1, 2, 3)

- Hide a loudly ticking clock in the room for a volunteer to find. Alternatively, invite a child to hide and blow a whistle. Ask children to help by keeping quiet so that the seeker can hear the sounds. (PD1, 2, 3, 7)

Creative Development

- Sing the 'Sound song' from *Game Songs with Prof Dogg's Troupe.* Help children to echo sounds using voices, body percussion and musical instruments. (C2, 5)

- Make sounds for children to guess using things around the room or body sounds. Go behind a screen or ask them to shut their eyes so they can concentrate on listening. Try clapping hands, shaking keys, tearing paper, bouncing a ball, tapping a pencil on a table, stamping feet on the floor. Invite children to make sounds for the others to identify. (C2, 3, 5)

- Try drawing and painting to music. Choose contrasting moods of music to inspire different styles of painting. (C1, 3, 5)

Activity: How do your ears work?

Learning opportunity: Investigating how well our ears work in different situations.

Early Learning Goal: Knowledge and Understanding of the World. Children will ask questions about why things happen and how things work.

Resources: *The Best Ears in the World* by Claire Llewellyn (optional); diagram of the inner ear; cardboard; scissors; sticky tape; blindfold; drum; rice; triangle.

Organisation: Whole group for circle game and book, small groups for investigations.

Key vocabulary: Ears, sounds, vibrate, drum, near, faraway, safe, danger.

What to do:

Sit in a circle and play Chinese whispers. Does the message stay the same as it passes from ear to ear? How does the ear hear the sounds?

Look at a diagram of the inner ear and point out the eardrum and all the tiny bones. Put a few grains of rice on the drum skin and ask a child to tap the drum gently. Watch the rice jump up and down as the drum vibrates. Explain that this creates a sound wave that travels through the air to our ears, along the tiny bones to the eardrum which also vibrates.

Read *The Best Ears in the World*. Investigate how far away we can hear sounds. Ask a child to go to the other end of the room and whisper a message. Who can hear what was said? Help children to make ear trumpets from cones of cardboard. Do they make it easier to hear the whisper? Go outside with a small group of children and a triangle. Ask a child to play the triangle nearby and then move away five steps and play it again. Keep doing this until the other children cannot hear the sound any more. Try with other sounds. Does everybody hear the same?

Activity: Musical moves

Learning opportunity: Playing cooperatively and using sounds/music to develop movement and coordination.

Early Learning Goal: Physical Development. Children will be able to move with confidence, imagination and in safety. They will show awareness of space, of themselves and of others.

Resources: Large space; percussion instruments; music for different moods, such as Barber's *Adagio for Strings*, blues songs (sad); Holst's *Jupiter, Turkish Rondo*, (Mozart), dance music (happy); *Moonlight Sonata* (Beethoven), music by Philip Glass (calm); *Mars* (Holst), Stravinsky's *Rite of Spring* (angry); *Danse Macabre* (Saint Saen), film music/soundtracks (scary).

Organisation: Whole group.

Key vocabulary: Skip, run, hop, freeze, mood, sad, happy, calm, angry, scary.

What to do:

Ask children to find a space in the room and stand completely still. Introduce different sound signals and let children suggest movements for each one, such as triangle = skip, claves = hop, tambourine = freeze! Practise moving when they hear each sound and freezing between each movement. Try making a sequence of sounds and moves for them to copy.

Develop the game by introducing mood music. Work with children to create happy, sad, calm, angry and scary dances.

Display

Make an interactive display. Record children's favourite sounds on a tape. Set up a tape recorder with headphones for others to listen to the sounds. Create a giant collage using drawings and paintings of ears and photos cut out of magazines. Mount the children's shell poems in shell shapes and display around the room. Hang the shell up so others can listen to the sounds inside!

Week 3

Touching hands

Personal, Social and Emotional Development

- Make a giant feely box. Cover each side of a cube with a different texture such as velvet, corrugated card, sandpaper, silver foil, wool, lace, plastic, leather, bubble wrap and so on. Make a hole in one side of the box and put in different items for children to identify by touch. (PS1, 2, 8)

- Make a touch board with sandpaper on one half and a smooth polished surface on the other. Invite children to feel the contrast with their eyes closed. Go on a touching walk outside. Use fingers to feel different textures - floors, walls, pavements, bricks, manhole covers, and so on. Make rubbings to record the patterns. (PS1, 2, 4, 8, 11)

- Practise dressing skills. How many children can fasten their own coat or put on their own shoes? Make a chart to encourage children. (PS1, 4, 10)

Communication, Language and Literacy

- Explore a variety of touch books such as Usborne's *Touchy Feely Books*. Make your own class book about favourite things to touch, such as animals (fun fur), warm towel after bath time (towelling), sandpit (sandpaper), squidgy dough (piece of dough sealed under cling-film), presents (bubble wrap) and so on. (L5, 7, 14, 16)

- Practise writing names in shallow trays of dry and wet sand. Use fingers to make patterns and letter shapes. Try with lentils, mud, custard powder or cornflour and water. (L16, 17, 18)

- Collect words to describe touch and textures - hot, cold, wet, dry, rough, smooth, soft, hard, fluffy, sticky. Scribe them on different sorts of paper and mount them on the wall. (L2, 7, 8)

- Make textured letters or numbers for children to trace with their fingers. (L11, 12)

Mathematical Development

- Put ten wooden cubes and ten round beads in a small cloth bag. Ask children to sort them into two piles without looking. Repeat with four shells, four coins, four buttons and four dice. (M1, 2)

- Make a collection of paired objects, such as bottle tops, paper clips, marbles, stones, buttons and acorns. Take two bags and put one of each object into a bag. Ask children to find matching pairs. One child picks an object from their bag and their partner has to find the pair. Try it with gloves on! Does that make it harder? (M1, 2, 11)

- Try tray puzzles blindfolded. (M8, 9, 10)

Knowledge and Understanding of the World

- Investigate which part of the body is most sensitive (see activity opposite). (K1, 2, 3, 4)

- Look at fingerprints under a magnifying glass and observe how they are all different. Use lipstick to make fingerprints. Blow them up on a photocopier and compare the patterns. (K3, 7)

Physical Development

- Make playdough or salt dough. Add beans, lentils, pasta, buttons or sequins to change the texture. Press different items such as tools, shells and leaves into the dough to make patterns. (PD8)

- Ask children to find a partner and sing 'We all clap hands together' from *This Little Puffin*. Invite children to clap their own hands and their partner's hands. Change actions to shake hands, rub noses, have a hug, and so on. (PD2, 3)

- Sit down facing a friend and sing:
  Hold, hold, hold my hands
  Rocking to and fro
  Backwards and forwards
  Round the world we go.
  (Tune: 'Row, row, row the boat') (PD2,3,5)

Creative Development

- Mix washing-up liquid into paint to make thick finger paint. Let children enjoy the feel of it on their fingers. Make textured paint by adding sand or lentils. Encourage the use of single thumb and finger prints as well as whole hands. (C1, 3)

- Try press printing with different natural and made objects, such as sponges, corks, plastic bricks, shells, pine cones, fruit and vegetables. (C1, 3)

- Make 'Touch squares' (see activity opposite). (C1, 3, 5)

Activity: Can you feel it?

Learning opportunity: Investigating which part of the body is most sensitive to touch.

Early Learning Goal: Knowledge and Understanding of the World. Children will find out about, and identify, some features of living things, objects and events they observe.

Resources: Feathers; paper clips; felt pens; paper; pencils; blindfold.

Organisation: Small group.

Key vocabulary: Feel, touch, tickle, palm, back, hand, cheek, arm, leg.

What to do:

Explain to children that you are going to find out which parts of the body are most sensitive to touch. Ask them to work with a partner and tickle each other with a feather on the palm and back of the hand. Try the cheek, ear, arm and leg. Which place feels the most ticklish? Is everyone the same?

Use a paper clip bent into a 'U' shape with the tips 2cm apart. Ask children to close their eyes and touch them on the palm of the hand. Can they feel one or two points touch them? Push the points closer together until they can feel only one point. Try on the arm or leg. The more sensitive parts of the body should still feel two points even when they are very close together. Record the results on a chart.

Play 'How close was that?'. Ask for a volunteer to wear a blindfold. Gently touch their hand with a red pen and make a mark. Ask them to use a contrasting colour pen and touch the same place. Remove the blindfold. How close together are the spots? Try again on different parts of the body.

Activity: Touch squares

Learning opportunity: Using a variety of materials to create a 3-d patchwork collage.

Early Learning Goal: Creative Development. Children will express and communicate their ideas, thoughts and feelings by using a wide range of materials and suitable tools.

Resources: Stiff cardboard or plywood cut into 30cm squares; straws; lolly sticks; collage materials (such as cotton wool balls, feathers, sand, rocks, twigs, wood, paper, fabric, beans, pasta, string, wool, rice, leaves, silver foil); glue; spray varnish.

Organisation: Small group.

Key vocabulary: Square, touch, names of materials, shiny, smooth, rough, soft, hard, cold, scratchy, tickly, blindfold.

What to do:

Allow children time to handle all the different materials and investigate the textures they like. Invite them to bring in suitable materials from home. Ask them to select a variety of contrasting textures to include in their collage boxes.

Help children to prepare the squares by subdividing them into six or nine smaller squares using art straws or lolly sticks. Ask them to stick a different texture into each square. Can they find words to describe each small square?

Ask for a volunteer to wear a blindfold. Can they identify the different materials in a friend's touch square using just their sense of touch?

Display

Make a collection of interesting natural objects to touch such as shells, stones, leaves, fur, leather and sponge. Invite children to handle them carefully and label with suitable describing words. Under the title 'What's inside?' make another collection of things which have a different texture on the outside from the inside (such as crusty bread, oranges, coconuts, soft-centred sweets, bananas, cherries and eggs). Ask children to write double-sided labels describing the textures. For example, 'On the outside I am hard, on the inside I am soft'.

Build a giant patchwork touch wall using the children's touch squares or cut out brick shapes and decorate them with different textures. Print thin borders for the displays using hand and foot prints.

Week 4

Teach children not to smell or taste strange things unless an adult has told them it is safe to do so.

Smelling noses

Personal, Social and Emotional Development

- Talk about how our sense of smell can warn us of possible dangers and keep us safe. What would the children do if they smelled smoke? If something smells bad should they eat or drink it? (PS1, 2, 4, 9, 12)

- Organise a 'Smelly socks day' (see activity opposite). (PS1, 4, 8, 9, 10)

Communication, Language and Literacy

- Read *Who's Making that Smell?* by Philip Hawthorn. Lift the flaps and enjoy guessing what the smell is each time. Talk about smells the children like and don't like. (L3, 4, 5, 7, 9)

- Write a group poem entitled 'I like the smell of ...' Talk about favourite smells to use in the poem, such as fresh air, clean clothes, fresh bread, cake, chocolate, flowers, peppermint. Change to nasty smells, such as dirty socks, medicine, toilets, wet hair, burnt toast, coffee. Do children agree on which smells they don't like? (L2, 3, 4, 5, 8)

- Read *The Three Little Wolves and the Big Bad Pig* by Eugene Trivizas. How do nice smells help the pig become good? (L3, 4, 6, 14)

Mathematical Development

- Make smelly playdough following this recipe:
  2 cups of flour   food colouring
  2 cups of water   3 tsp cream of tartar
  1 cup of salt   1 tbsp vegetable oil
  2 drops of one of these: peppermint oil, carnation or other flower oil, orange oil, mixed spice or cinnamon

  Heat all the ingredients in a saucepan, stirring until they blend into a thick dough. Use number cards and ask children to make two flowers, four gingerbrcad mcn, and so on. (M1, 2, 3)

- Make a bar chart of most and least favourite smells. Which is the most popular? (M1, 2, 4, 11)

- Let children make smelly spells and potions in the water tray using safe herbs and spices (such as cinnamon, cumin, ginger, mixed spice), coloured water, different sized bottles with lids, teaspoons, pipettes, bowls and so on. Can they name, label and price their creations? (M1, 3, 11, 12)

Knowledge and Understanding of the World

- Make a collection of strong smells for children to sniff. Can they recognise lemon, banana, mint, garlic, chocolate, coffee, roses, pencil shavings, vinegar, sawdust, ginger? Ask them to close their eyes or use a blindfold. Which smells do they like and not like? (K1, 2, 3, 4, 11)

- Play 'Smelly matching pairs'. Put matching smells in plastic lidded containers. Can the children find two that smell the same? (K1, 3)

- Read *Whose Nose and Toes?* by John Butler. Draw and paint pictures of animals with special noses and toes. (K2, 3, 9)

Physical Development

- Move around the room like elephants (see activity opposite). (PD2, 3, 7)

- Go on a smelling walk, inside and outside. Talk about nice and nasty smells. Can children recognise all the smells? Try to smell flowers, leaves, fresh air, traffic, dustbins, fresh laundry, cooking, rain, soap, and so on. (PD1, 2, 3)

- Try some deep breathing exercises. Standing up tall, breathe in and out slowly. Remind children not to scrunch up their shoulders. Try holding breath for a count of three or five. To help children breathe in properly ask them to pretend to sniff a sweet flower or cup of delicious hot chocolate. What happens if you ask them to sniff a smelly sock or mouldy tomato? They could breathe out quickly and pull a disgusted face! Ask them to run around the room until you give them a signal to stop. What has happened to their breathing now? (PD3, 4, 5)

Creative Development

- Add perfume, aromatherapy oil, coffee or spices to paint. (Discourage children from sniffing harmful substances.) Do their paintings still smell when they are dry? (C1, 3)

- Make pot-pourri using a selection of materials such as coloured pasta, lavender, pine cones, wood shavings, dried flowers, bay leaves, rosemary, dried citrus peel and aromatherapy oils. Put into small plastic bags and fasten with ribbons. (C3, 5)

● Make scratch and sniff cards using dried herbs (such as oregano, basil, and rosemary) or spices and dried flowers. (C3, 4, 5)

Activity: Smelly socks day

Learning opportunity: Sharing the benefit of wearing clean clothes, washing socks and polishing shoes.

Early Learning Goal: Personal, Social and Emotional Development. Children will have a developing awareness of their own needs, views and feelings and be sensitive to the needs, views and feelings of others. They will be able to dress and undress independently.

Resources: Children's own pairs of dirty socks; water tray; mild soap powder; rubber gloves; washing line; pegs; washboard; mangle; ironing board; iron; shoes; polish; brushes; dusters.

Organisation: Whole group for introduction, small groups for washing activities.

Key vocabulary: Smell, clean, dirty, soap, bubbles, rub, polish, wring, wet, dry.

What to do:

Explain that you are going to hold a 'Smelly socks day' and invite children to bring in a pair of socks to wash. Talk about the smells they are likely to experience - dirty feet, mud, soap, clean laundry.

Set up a laundry area in the role-play corner with warm soapy water in the water tray and washing boards so that the children can rub their socks clean. Provide rubber gloves for children with sensitive skin. Use a basin with clean water to rinse out the soap. Help children to wring their socks, put them through the mangle, and hang them up to dry. Talk about how, in the past, before washing machines, all clothes washing was done like this.

Open a shoe shine stall so that children can learn how to polish and enjoy the smell of clean shoes. Offer this as a service to parents when they come to fetch children at the end of the session and at the 'Senses factory' (see Week 6).

Activity: Goodness gracious what a nose!

Learning opportunity: Moving around the room like elephants, balancing and responding to music.

Early Learning Goal: Physical Development. Children will be able to move with control and coordination. They will travel around, under, over and through balancing and climbing equipment.

Resources: Large space; *This Little Puffin*; 'The Elephant' from *Carnival of the Animals* by Saint Saens; skipping ropes; playground chalk; balancing beams.

Organisation: Whole group.

Key vocabulary: Words of the rhyme, big, slow, trunk, nose, balancing.

What to do:

Ask children to find a space. Sing and act out the rhyme 'An elephant goes like this and that', from *This Little Puffin*. How big can they make their bodies? Can they make their arms into long trunks.

Listen to 'The Elephant'. Ask children to move around the room as they imagine an elephant would move. Collect words to describe the movement - slow, lumbering, swinging, careful, plodding and so on.

Teach children the song 'One grey elephant balancing' from *This Little Puffin*. Stretch out skipping ropes on the floor for children to balance on step by step as they sing. How many elephants can balance on each rope? Draw a spider's web shape on the floor using chalk and assemble all the elephants together to balance. What happens if the web breaks?

Display

Take photographs of children on 'Smelly socks day' doing all the different activities. Mount and display them for parents to see. Ask children to draw and write about the day on sock-shaped pieces of paper. Hang their work on a washing line with clothes pegs.

Week 5
Tasting tongues

Personal, Social and Emotional Development

- Read *Oliver's Fruit Salad* by Vivian French. Share a variety of fruit with children. Encourage them to try some more unusual tastes like kiwi fruit and pomegranates. Let children talk about the tastes they like and don't like. Make a giant fruit salad to share for a snack. (PS1, 2, 4, 8)

- Grow cherry tomatoes or radishes in grow bags for children to try different tastes. Draw up a rota to help with watering. (PS1, 6, 7, 8)

Communication, Language and Literacy

- Make a collection of words to describe tastes - hot, cold, sour, sweet, bitter, spicy, bland, tasty, nasty, sickly, scrumptious, delicious, tangy, smoky, salty, crispy, and so on. Encourage children to use these words at snack and meal times. (L1, 2, 4, 8)

- Read or tell the traditional story of 'The Gingerbread Man' (see activity opposite). (L1, 3, 4, 5, 14)

- Write recipes and menus for the Tasty Café. (L16, 18, 19)

Mathematical Development

- Open a café in the role-play area. Plan different menus, such as sweet, savoury, fruit, healthy, chocolate and celebration. Make, buy and sell food in the café. Ask children to take on the roles of waiter, chef, customer, manager. (M1, 2, 3, 5)

- Play 'Eat the pie' (see activity opposite). (M2, 3, 9, 10)

- Sing lots of tasty number rhymes, such as 'Ten fat sausages', 'Five fat peas', 'Five currant buns'. Can children make up new food rhymes? (M1, 2, 3, 4)

- Sprinkle cress seeds onto paper towels in the shape of different numbers. How many numbers can they grow? Water regularly and then eat the cress in sandwiches or add to a salad for a snack. (M3)

Knowledge and Understanding of the World

- Put a small amount of flour, caster sugar, salt and icing sugar into four containers. Ask children to dip a finger into each powder, taste and describe the contents. Try matching pairs by having four pairs of powders for children to taste and match. (K1, 2, 4)

- Make your own fizzy sherbet. Crush together 6 tsp of citric acid crystals (available from most chemist's) with 3 tsp of baking powder (soda) in a small bowl or pestle and mortar to make a fine powder. Mix in 4 tsp of icing sugar and put in a jar. Ask children to dip a finger in the powder and put it on their tongue. What does it feel and taste like? (K1, 2, 4, 5)

- Make some tasty food for the café. Use strong flavours. Try peppermint creams or chocolate brownies, tomato soup or anchovy pizza. (K1, 3, 6, 7)

- Make a collection of tastes from around the world for children to try at snack time, such as French bread, Greek olives, Italian pizza, Indian pakora, Chinese noodles, American hotdogs and Spanish oranges. (K1, 9, 10)

Physical Development

- Use empty food packets, boxes and containers to build large-scale models such as walls, castles, machines and vehicles. (PD6, 8)

- Choose four contrasting tastes, such as pizza, fish and chips, chicken nuggets and soup and draw them on sets of cards. Chant the words on the cards and clap the word rhythms. Ask children to clap or chant their word as they move around the room. Can they find anyone else with the same taste in food? (PD1, 3, 7)

Creative Development

- Give each child an A4 card sandwich box. Invite them to draw or stick on pictures of tasty and healthy food for their lunch. Sing 'What would you like in your lunch box?', to the tune of 'What shall we do with the drunken sailor?'. (C1, 2, 5)

- Make favourite meals by gluing collage materials onto paper plates. Try sponge chips, brown corduroy sausages, tissue paper peas and so on. Use to decorate the walls of the café. (C5)

Activity: The gingerbread man

Learning opportunity: Retelling the story of 'The gingerbread man' to explore drama and cooking.

Early Learning Goal: Communication, Language and Literacy. Children will listen with enjoyment and respond to stories, songs and other music, rhymes and poems and make up their own stories, songs, rhymes and poems. They will use language to imagine and recreate roles and experiences.

Resources: Any version of the traditional story 'The gingerbread man'; gingerbread men cookie cutters; ingredients (250g plain flour, 125g butter or margarine, 125g dark brown sugar, 1 small egg, pinch of salt, 2 tsp of either mixed spice, ground ginger or cinnamon *or* a few drops of vanilla essence/ peppermint oil *or* the juice and zest of half a lemon or orange *or* 50g of cocoa).

Organisation: Whole group to listen to story; small groups to act it out and cook.

Key vocabulary: Words used in 'The gingerbread man' story, biscuit, names of ingredients and different flavours.

What to do:

Read or tell children the traditional story of 'The gingerbread man' who ran away to avoid being eaten! Help children to choose different parts of the story to retell and act out. Everyone can join in the refrain 'Run, run, as fast as you can. You can't catch me, I'm the gingerbread man'.

Explain that you are going to make your own gingerbread men biscuits but there is a choice of flavours and tastes - spicy, cinnamon, ginger, lemon, orange, chocolate, vanilla or peppermint! Try to make some of each so children can compare tastes.

Beat the butter and sugar together until soft and add the beaten egg gradually. Add the sieved flour, salt and chosen flavouring. Mix into a firm dough and chill in the fridge for 30 minutes. Roll out on a floured surface until 0.5 cm thick. Cut out shapes and cook on a greased baking tray for 12-15 minutes at gas mark 5, 190 C

Activity: Eat the pie

Learning opportunity: Playing a cooperative game to develop recognition of colours and numbers.

Early Learning Goal: Mathematical Development. Children will be able to recognise numerals from one to nine. They will use language, such as 'circle' or 'bigger', to describe the shape and size of solid and flat shapes.

Resources: Paper plates; six coloured segments of card for each child; rulers; pencils; pens; dice.

Organisation: Small group.

Key vocabulary: Pie, circle, numbers one to six, colours, turn, slice, segment, piece.

What to do:

Explain that you are going to play a game using colours and numbers called 'Eat the pie'. Give each child a circular paper plate and help them to divide it into six segments. Write the numbers one to six on the slices.

Ask children to choose six different coloured segments of card and number them one to six. Place them on top of the corresponding numbers on their plate. Take turns to throw the dice and remove or 'eat' that slice of pie. The winner is the first to eat their whole pie. Encourage children to identify shapes, numbers and colours and use mathematical language as they play the game.

Display

Set up an interactive display called 'Only the nose knows'. Invite children to distinguish between the taste of apples and pears while holding their nose. Can they taste the difference?

Paint a giant picture of 'The gingerbread man' and ask children to draw pictures and write about the biscuits they made. Use the cookie cutters to print shapes on thin strips of paper to make borders for the display. Try printing with fruit and vegetables using bright paint on black sugar paper. Use potatoes, carrots, cauliflower, apples, pears, oranges and star fruit.

Week 6

Working together

Personal, Social and Emotional Development

- Talk about how the senses work together to tell us about the world and keep us safe. Go on a senses walk around the local area. Point out how children are using different senses as they look at their environment, listen to sounds, smell traffic and pick up leaves. (PS2, 4, 6, 9, 12)

- Introduce the idea of the 'Senses factory' that will take place this week. What preparations do children need to make? Which of the activities would children like to share? (PS1, 4, 7, 8, 11)

- Play 'Which sense?' (see activity opposite). (PS1, 3, 8)

Communication, Language and Literacy

- Take a head and shoulders photograph of each child. Let the children label their sense organs. Ask each child to complete a caption for their photo 'My favourite sense is ...'. (L16, 17, 18)

- Write invitations to parents, carers, friends and local schools to visit the 'Senses factory'. Make posters to advertise the event. (L15, 16, 17, 19)

- Tell a story using all the senses or describe the senses walk. Give out cards for each sense. When children hear their sense ask them to hold up the card. (L3, 6, 7, 9, 12)

Mathematical Development

- Give each child a simple outline of a figure. Ask them to draw in all the sense organs and count and label how many eyes, ears, noses, tongues and fingers they have drawn. (M1, 2, 3)

- Involve children in planning the games for the 'Senses factory' such as 'Guess the number of sweets in a jar'. (M1, 2, 11)

- Make giant numerals using ribbon, rope, chains, construction toys, and so on. (M1, 3)

Knowledge and Understanding of the World

- Buy a whole fresh fish, such as mackerel or trout. Let children look at the scales through a magnifying glass, touch it and smell it. Cook the fish and see how the smell changes. Enjoy the taste of eating the fish. Which sense did they not use? Ask children to record what they thought on a simple writing frame (see below). (K1, 2, 3, 4)

	before cooking	after cooking
sight		
hearing		
touch		
smell		
taste		

- Make bread. (K1, 2, 3, 4)

- Go on a bug hunt outside. Observe small creatures using magnifying glasses and bug boxes. Handle them carefully. Investigate how other creatures see, hear and feel. Draw around each child's hand and let them draw on a picture of their minibeast. (K1, 2, 3, 9)

Physical Development

- Draw large symbols for each sense on the ground using chalk. Ask children to run to the correct symbol in response to your questions. 'Which sense am I using when I ... read a book/eat an apple/have a bath/listen to music?'. Some activities may use more than one sense. (PD1, 3)

- Work with clay or wood (see opposite). (PD8)

- Talk about how using our senses keeps us healthy. What happens when one sense doesn't work properly? (PD4)

Creative Development

- Paint self-portraits. Let children look in small mirrors and paint their faces. Don't forget the ears! Frame or laminate some of the paintings. Provide laminated sets of labels for the eyes, ears, mouth, nose and hands using a computer and let children stick them onto their pictures. (C1)

- Act out the story of 'Little Red Riding Hood', when the crafty wolf uses all his senses to try and catch a tasty meal! (C4)

- Make musical instruments that are good to look at, make interesting sounds and have different textures to feel. Make shakers using clear, ridged squash bottles filled with coloured beads, sequins and feathers. Shake, rattle and scrape to make sounds. (C4, 5)

Activity: Which sense?

Learning opportunity: Sharing a game. Developing and assessing children's understanding of how different senses work.

Early Learning Goal: Personal, Social and Emotional Development. Children will work as part of a group or class, taking turns and sharing fairly.

Resources: Collection of items or pictures to represent each sense, such as light bulb, torch (sight); musical instrument, CD (hearing); socks, soap (smell); apple, ice-cream (taste); glove, feather (touch); five pieces of card with the name of a different sense written on each; five plastic hoops.

Organisation: Whole group.

Key vocabulary: Names of items and senses, turn.

What to do:

Ask children to sit in a circle. Place the items you have collected in the middle with the five labelled hoops. Ask children to work together to sort the items into the hoops. Check that children can say why they think that is the right sense to use.

Choose some items that use more than one sense to challenge children's thinking such as food, flowers, animals. Invite children to find other items or pictures to include. A version of this game could be transferred to a table top for an interactive display or game at the 'Senses factory'.

Activity: The clay factory

Learning opportunity: Using all the senses to handle and work with clay or wood.

Early Learning Goal: Physical Development. Children will handle tools, objects, construction and malleable materials safely and with increasing control.

Resources: A handful of clay for each child; clay tools; clay tiles or boards; items to press into clay; clay models, sculptures or pictures; small pots of water.

Organisation: Small group.

Key vocabulary: Clay, work, squeeze, soften, roll, flatten, twist, press, pot.

What to do:

Invite children to feel and describe the clay (cold, damp, hard) as they begin to work. Show how to soften the clay by dropping it onto a hard surface. They can squeeze it in their hands and flatten it by hitting the clay with the palm of the hand; poke holes in it with fingers and draw lines with fingernails; roll into worm shapes and flatten with rolling pins; smooth the surface of the clay with water.

Ask children to smell the clay on their hands. Does the smell change when the clay is wet? Ask them to listen, as they work with the clay, to the sounds it makes.

Encourage children to flatten the clay into tiles or leaf shapes using the palms of their hands and use tools to make patterns. They can scratch their names or initials into the clay. Make pinch pots using a small ball of clay. Push the thumb into the ball to make a hole and pinch the clay all around the edges between the finger and thumb. Tap on the board to flatten the base. Rub with water to smooth the sides and insides. Make simple animal sculptures of hedgehogs or snails.

Adapt the pinch pots to become candle or tea-light holders. Decorate with pasta, beads and pressed patterns and spray silver or gold.

Display

Mount and display the children's favourite sense photographs in a gallery for parents to see at the 'Senses factory'. Make a cardboard model of a child to stand and welcome visitors. On thick card draw round a child, with their hand extended, to point at the entrance, paint on clothes and cut out.

Bringing it all together

Explain to children that in a few days time you're going to be holding a special event. They can show their friends and families their work on the senses by opening a 'Senses factory'. Encourage children to think about some of the songs, activities, games and investigations they have enjoyed. What would they like to show their visitors? How could they ask them to join in?

Preparation

Talk about making invitations and posters to advertise the 'Senses factory'. What information will people need to know? Who will they choose to invite? Don't forget to send invitations to local schools and nursery groups. Adult help will be essential to the success of this event. Support will be needed in setting up activities, serving refreshments, manning stalls, taking photographs and helping children to enjoy the activities.

Rehearse the songs and drama that the children choose to show their visitors.

Refreshments

Ask children to think about which food would be suitable to serve at the 'Senses factory'. This could include:

- Homemade bread (see Week 6)
- Gingerbread men biscuits (see Week 5)
- Tastes from around the world (see Week 5)
- Noisy snacks: crisps, apples, raw carrots and celery, crackers and cheese

- Brightly coloured drinks: pink lemonade (add blackcurrant cordial to lemonade), blue apple juice (add a few drops of food colouring!)

Activities

Set up five different sense stations around the room for children and their families to visit.

Sight: microscope, kaleidoscope, magnifying glass, prism, mirror. Invite parents to touch Braille books and embossed patterns children have created (see Week 1).

Hearing: bells, whistles, other musical instruments, spoons, CD player. Demonstrate the homemade telephone and listening tube. Play 'Musical moves' (see Week 2).

Touch: sandpaper, clay, dough, ice, finger paints, trays of sand or lentils. Display the children's feely boxes. Play 'Matching pairs' (see Week 3).

Smell: vanilla essence, perfume, flowers, chocolate, spices. Use smelly playdough and play 'Smelly matching pairs' (see Week 4).

Taste: jelly beans, fruit salad, salty crisps, pickles, tomatoes. Play 'Eat the pie' (see Week 5).

Games and stalls

Here are some more ideas for games and stalls that could be included in the 'Senses factory'. If a small entry charge is made, funds could be raised for your setting. Alternatively, you may decide to raise funds for a suitable charity.

- Guessing games: guess the number of jelly beans in a jar, the weight of a teddy bear, how many glass beads on a tray.
- Invite parents to buy framed self-portraits or photographs of their children (see Week 6).
- Sell pot-pourri bags and scratch-and-sniff cards (see Week 4).
- Display and sell clay models (see Week 6).
- Set up a shoe shine stall so visitors can have their shoes cleaned (see Week 4).

Follow-up activities

Ask visitors to fill in an evaluation sheet to show which was their favourite part of the 'Senses factory'. Children can look through them and find out which game or stall was the most popular. Put up on display enlarged photographs taken on the day of children involved in all the different activities. Ask children to compose suitable captions for them using a computer.

Resources

Resources to collect

- Large poster of child.
- Glasses frames.
- Senses books, puzzles, posters and games.
- Braille books.
- Magnifying glasses, microscope, binoculars, mirrors.
- Shape sorters.
- Large shell.
- Story tapes.
- Small jingle bells.
- Small cloth bags.
- Small items for feely boxes.
- Mangle, pegs and washing line.
- Aromatherapy oils.
- Spices - cinnamon, cumin, ginger, and so on.
- Food magazines.
- Grow bags and tomato seeds or plants.
- Empty squash bottles.

Everyday resources

- Tissue boxes, cardboard tubes, plastic cups, film canisters, plastic bottles and containers, tins, art straws, paper plates, string, and glue for modelling.
- Paper and card of different weights, colours and textures (such as sugar paper, corrugated card, sandpaper, silver and shiny paper).
- Dry powder paints for mixing and ready-mixed paint for covering large areas and printing.
- Different-sized paintbrushes, from household brushes and rollers to thin brushes for intricate work, and a variety of paint-mixing containers.
- Extra collage material such as lentils, beans, sequins, pasta, buttons, feathers, bubble wrap, cotton wool balls, different textured fabric (fun fur, velvet, towelling, blanket).
- Softwood, hammers, nails, lolly sticks, bottle tops, paper clips and nails, for woodwork.
- Salt and playdough ingredients and cutters.
- Glove and finger puppets.
- CD/tape recorder and musical instruments.
- Role-play equipment for optician's and Tasty Café

Stories

Lucy's Picture by Nicola Moon (Orchard).

Duck's Key, Where can it be? by Jez Alborough (Collins).

That's not my Teddy by Fiona Watt and Rachel Wells *Touchy Feely Books* (Usborne).

Who's Making that Smell? by Philip Hawthorn (Usborne).

The Three Little Wolves and the Big Bad Pig by Eugene Trivizas (Heinemann).

Whose Nose and Toes? by John Butler (Puffin).

Oliver's Fruit Salad by Vivian French (Hodder).

The Smelly Book by Babette Cole (Red Fox).

Woolly's Walk by Stephen Cartwright *Touchy Feely Books* (Usborne).

Kipper's Sticky Paws Touch and Feel Books by Mick Inkpen (Red Wagon).

Supersenses by Dr Seuss (Collins).

Spot's Touch and Feel Day by Eric Hill (Putmans).

Hello Ocean by Pam Munoz Ryan (Charlesbridge).

Non-fiction

The Best Ears in the World by Claire Llewellyn (Hodder).

How do your Senses Work? by Alastair Smith *Flip flap* series (Usborne).

Senses by Angela Royston (Heinemann).

The Five Senses by Herve Tullet (Tate Publishing).

The Senses by David Glover (Franklin Watts).

Songs and rhymes

Game Songs with Prof Dogg's Troupe chosen by Harriet Powell (A and C Black).

This Little Puffin by Elizabeth Matterson (Puffin).

Bobby Shaftoe, Clap your Hands by Sue Nicholls (A and C Black).

Bingo Lingo by Helen Macgregor (A and C Black).

Me compiled by Ana Sanderson (A and C Black).

Collecting evidence of children's learning

Monitoring children's development is an important task. Keeping a record of children's achievements will help you to see progress and will draw attention to those who are having difficulties for some reason. If a child needs additional professional help, such as speech therapy, your records will provide valuable evidence.

Records should be the result of collaboration between group leaders, parents and carers. Parents should be made aware of your record keeping policies when their child joins your group. Show them the type of records you are keeping and make sure they understand that they have an opportunity to contribute. As a general rule, your records should form an open document. Any parent should have access to records relating to his or her child. Take regular opportunities to talk to parents about children's progress. If you have formal discussions regarding children about whom you have particular concerns, a dated record of the main points should be kept.

Keeping it manageable

Records should be helpful in informing group leaders, adult helpers and parents and always be for the benefit of the child. However, keeping records of every aspect of each child's development can become a difficult task. The sample shown will help to keep records manageable and useful. The golden rule is to keep them simple.

Observations will basically fall into three categories:

● **Spontaneous records:** Sometimes you will want to make a note of observations as they happen, for example a child is heard counting cars accurately during a play activity, or is seen to play collaboratively for the first time.

● **Planned observations:** Sometimes you will plan to make observations of children's developing skills

in their everyday activities. Using the learning opportunity identified for an activity will help you to make appropriate judgments about children's capabilities and to record them systematically.

To collect information:

- talk to children about their activities and listen to their responses;

- listen to children talking to each other;

- observe children's work such as early writing, drawings, paintings and 3-d models. (Keeping photocopies or photographs is sometimes useful.)

Sometimes you may wish to set up one-off activities for the purposes of monitoring development. Some groups, for example, ask children to make a drawing of themselves at the beginning of each term to record their progressing skills in both coordination and observation. Do not attempt to make records following every activity!

● **Reflective observations:** It is useful to spend regular time reflecting on the progress of a few children (about four) each week. Aim to make some brief comments about each child every half term.

Informing your planning

Collecting evidence about children's progress is time-consuming but essential. When you are planning, use the information you have collected to help you to decide what learning opportunities you need to provide next for children. For example, a child who has poor pencil or brush control will benefit from more play with dough or construction toys to build the strength of hand muscles.

Example of recording chart

Name: Luca Robinson		DOB 19.7.01		Date of entry: 29.9.04		
Term	Personal, Social and Emotional Development	Communication, Language and Literacy	Mathematical Development	Knowledge and Understanding of the World	Physical Development	Creative Development
ONE	Reluctant to leave carer and speak to other adults Hesitant to try new activities 5.10.04 EB	Talks to himself as he plays Enjoys listening to stories, esp *Who's Making that Smell?* 18.10.04 GS	Can say numbers to ten and count accurately ten objects Knows colours and some shapes 12.10.04 EB	Enjoyed making feely box, Made suggestions for what to put inside 7.11.04 GS	Lacks confidence on large apparatus Good control of tools 21.11.04 RA	Wary of paint and messy activities Reluctant to sing 3.12.04 EB

Skills overview of six-week plan

Week	Topic focus	Personal, Social and Emotional Development	Communication, Language and Literacy	Mathematical Development	Knowledge and Understanding of the World	Physical Development	Creative Development
1	Seeing eyes	Taking turns Listening Discussing feelings	Role play Enjoying books Retelling stories Making books	Counting Estimating Matching pairs	Observing Investigating Constructing	Moving safely Throwing and catching	Singing Painting Designing and using materials
2	Hearing ears	Listening Taking turns Care of others	Rhyming Listening to stories Writing poems	Addition Subtraction Matching Counting	Investigating Constructing Using materials	Moving with imagination and control	Singing Making sounds Painting to music
3	Touching hands	Talking Taking turns Awareness of safety Dressing skills	Enjoying books Making books Writing names Extending vocab	Sorting Matching Puzzles	Investigating Observing	Using malleable materials Partner work	Finger painting Printing Using materials Collage
4	Smelling noses	Awareness of needs Planning as a group Taking turns Good relationships with adults	Enjoying books Making flap books Writing poems	Counting Measuring Bar charts Measuring and exploring volume	Asking questions Investigating Recording	Moving with imagination and awareness of space Recognising body changes	Painting Using materials
5	Tasting tongues	Listening Trying new activities Sharing Taking turns	Extending vocabulary Retelling stories Drama Writing menus	Money Recognising numbers Number rhymes	Investigating Constructing Cooking	Using a range of equipment Moving with control and awareness of space	Collage Using materials
6	Working together	Awareness of safety Collaborative planning Taking turns/Sharing Discussing feelings	Writing captions and invitations Listening Making up stories	Counting Estimating Recognising numbers	Investigating Cooking Observing environment	Moving with control and coordination Handling tools Keeping healthy	Singing Painting self-portraits Drama Making musical instruments

Home links

The theme of 'The senses' lends itself to useful links with children's homes and families. Through working together children and adults gain respect for each other and build comfortable and confident relationships.

Establishing partnerships

● Keep parents and carers informed about the topic and the themes for each week. They will enjoy contributing ideas, time and resources.

● Ask parents' permission before taking children out on any of the walks. Describe the planned route and explain the purpose of the walk. Invite parents to accompany you.

● Photocopy the parent's page for each child to take home.

● Invite parents and friends to visit the 'Senses factory' at the end of the topic.

Visiting enthusiasts

● Invite adults who play musical instruments to visit and play music for children to listen to.

● Contact your local branches of the Royal National Institute for the Blind and the Deaf and ask if representatives can visit and bring a working dog or show the children some sign language.

Resource requests

● Ask parents to donate old glasses frames (remove the lenses) or sunglasses, different textured materials and fabrics, an old-fashioned mangle and food magazines.

● Invite parents to contribute cushions and soft furnishings for the cosy listening area.

● Ask for volunteers to cook food from other cultures, favourite and national dishes, to bring in and share during Week 4, 'Tasting tongues'.

The senses factory

● It is always useful to have extra adults at special events to help with stalls, games, activities and refreshments and to encourage and support children.